Original title:
Crinkled Wisps Among the Mermaid Fang

Author: Paulina Pähkel
ISBN HARDBACK: 978-1-80562-387-8
ISBN PAPERBACK: 978-1-80563-908-4

Celestial Echoes Beneath the Tide

In the silent depths where the dreams drift slow,
Stars wander down where the soft currents flow.
Whispers of night in a watery embrace,
Crafting a ballet, a timeless grace.

In the ripples, tales of the moon's bright beam,
Dancing with shadows, the heart of a dream.
Echoes of starlight on fish's soft skin,
A shimmering world, where the stories begin.

Threads of Blue and Coral Light

Beneath the waves, where the colors entwine,
Coral giants bloom in a dance so divine.
The blue of the sea paints each moment anew,
Threads of life whisper in hues that we view.

With every sway, the ocean woos bright,
Under the waves, every secret ignites.
A tapestry woven from dreams and delight,
In the heart of the sea, threads shimmer and bite.

Catching Echoes in the Sea's Embrace

In the embrace of the sea, echoes are caught,
Secrets and songs in the ripples are sought.
Flotsam of memories drift close and subside,
Each wave a whisper, where dreams try to hide.

The tide pulls us gently, a lullaby's call,
Filling the air with a soft, soothing thrall.
Glimmers of sunlight dance over the foam,
In the sea's deep breath, we discover our home.

Flickering Shadows on the Ocean Floor

Glimmering shadows where the sea creatures play,
Flickers of life in a ballet of gray.
Each flicker a story, a moment in time,
Where the ocean sings softly, a silvery rhyme.

From beneath the waves, worlds start to unfold,
Shadows of dreams in the depths, quiet, bold.
Through the darkness, the light weaves a tale,
Flickering memories that drift without fail.

Twilight Dreams of the Sea Sprite

In twilight's glow, a sea sprite sighs,
Her whispers weave through soft, warm skies.
With glimmers bright, she softly glides,
Her laughter dances where mystery hides.

Upon the waves, the silver spark,
She twirls and spins, a shimmering arc.
Each wave tells tales of wonders past,
Her magic swirls, a spell she's cast.

The moonbeams kiss the ocean's face,
In gentle waves, she finds her place.
A quiet promise, her heart will keep,
For those who wander in dreams so deep.

A lullaby of the night takes flight,
Guiding lost souls with pure delight.
Her essence sparkles, a beacon rare,
In twilight's cloak, she whispers there.

With every tide, her secrets flow,
In twilight dreams, the soft winds blow.
A fleeting glimpse of the realm divine,
Where sea sprites dwell and stars align.

Flashing Colors Beneath the Surface

Beneath the waves, where colors gleam,
A world unfolds, a vibrant dream.
Coral castles in hues so bright,
Guarded by creatures of sheer delight.

A dance of fish, in brisk ballet,
With flickering tails, they twist and sway.
In playful arcs, they paint the deep,
Secrets hidden where shadows creep.

Anemones sway in the gentle flow,
With jeweled hearts in the ebb and glow.
Each heartbeat echoes, a poetic sound,
In depths where wonder and joy abound.

The starfish linger, the sea urchins roam,
In their muted colors, they find a home.
Flashes of beauty in every glance,
Invite us to join their silent dance.

Beneath the surface, a tale unwinds,
Of harmony woven in nature's designs.
A treasure trove in the ocean's embrace,
Where colors shimmer, and spirits race.

Dreamcatchers in Aquatic Realities

In the quiet depths they weave,
Bright strands of hope and dreams to cleave,
Beneath the waves, where silence sings,
A world awakens, soft as wings.

Moonlit shadows gently glide,
While shimmering fish in currents hide,
With tendrils spun from starlit grace,
They capture visions in their space.

A tranquil net, both strong and fine,
Draws forth the dreams that intertwine,
In coral gardens, magic grows,
Where vibrant life in rhythm flows.

Listen closely, hear the tales,
Of all the creatures, fins and scales,
Their stories swirl, a vibrant dance,
In currents strong, they find their chance.

With every tide, hope finds a way,
As darkness fades to break of day,
In aquatic realms, dreams rest and wait,
For hearts to find their destined fate.

Luminous Whirls in the Deep

In depths where shadows twist and churn,
The glow of wonders starts to turn,
A dance of light in ocean's arms,
With glimmers bright, entangled charms.

Swirling softly like the breeze,
They shimmer through the watery trees,
Each flicker tells a tale untold,
Of ancient secrets, brave and bold.

With bubbles rising, thoughts set free,
They spiral forth like waves from sea,
A tapestry of dreams unspun,
In luminous whirls, they come undone.

Here, echoes whisper through the blue,
The call of depths as tales ensue,
With laughter light, they intertwine,
In this enchanted realm, divine.

So let the currents guide your heart,
Into the magic where dreams start,
For in this dance of light and sea,
Awaits the truth of who you'll be.

Swaying Shadows in the Abyss

In the abyss where shadows sway,
The whispers of the night betray,
A hidden world of secrets deep,
Where silence holds what dreams can't keep.

Ghostly forms in delicate weave,
Entwine like tales that we believe,
Each flicker hints at ancient lore,
As swaying shadows softly bore.

Through currents dark, a path appears,
Guided by hopes, our hearts, our fears,
With every pulse, the ocean speaks,
Of hidden wonders, lost mystique.

A dance of echoes, spirits twirl,
In the depths where time can unfurl,
With hushed caresses, shadows weave,
An artful pattern we perceive.

In twilight's grip, we seek to find,
The deeper truths of what's defined,
For in the dark, a light might gleam,
From swaying shadows born of dream.

Driftwood Dreams and Ocean Whispers

Amidst the tides, driftwood lies,
A vessel shaped by sea and skies,
Each piece a tale, each curve a rhyme,
A whispered secret lost in time.

Beneath the moon, the waves converse,
With gentle songs, an ancient verse,
They carry dreams on breezes warm,
Of distant shores and thunderstorm.

With every crash, a story told,
Of sailors young and hearts of gold,
Their echoes dance through seashell's grace,
In ocean whispers, time leaves no trace.

As driftwood sways, it yearns to roam,
Each wave a step towards its home,
Adrift in currents, life takes flight,
Where dreams are born, and hearts ignite.

So gather 'round, beneath the stars,
Let whispers guide you near and far,
For driftwood dreams in twilight's glow,
Hold the secrets only the sea knows.

Sapphire Whispers Beneath the Stars

In twilight's hush, the whispers start,
Sapphire dreams that fill the heart.
Beneath the stars, the secrets gleam,
A moonlit dance, a silver dream.

With every glimmer, shadows play,
In this enchanted, twilight sway.
Each twinkle tells a tale so bright,
Of wishes whispered through the night.

A breeze that carries hope afar,
Dancing lightly among the stars.
Promises wrapped in silver threads,
Awakening where wonder spreads.

Ensnared in Ocean's Embrace

In depths where daylight dims its glow,
The ocean sings, soft and low.
Its arms enfold, a tender hold,
Where secrets of the deep unfold.

The waves caress with soothing hymn,
A melody both bright and dim.
Ensnared in tides, lost to the swell,
I drift in dreams, beneath the spell.

Coral castles fair and grand,
Whisper tales of timeless land.
Beneath the moon's embrace so bright,
I dance within the crystal light.

Fantasies of the Submerged Realm

In a realm where silence sings,
Fantasies take flight on wings.
Creatures weave through azure tides,
In dreams where magic gently hides.

Starfish twinkle like distant dreams,
While seaweed sways in gentle streams.
Whispers swirl in liquid air,
Creating worlds beyond compare.

A kingdom lost, yet never gone,
Where time is woven, dusk to dawn.
In depths adorned with shades so bright,
The heart finds solace in the night.

Lullabies of the Abyssal Wraith

Where shadows dance in depths unknown,
The wraith hums soft, a haunting tone.
Lullabies of sorrow, sweet,
In echoes where the lost souls meet.

With every wave, a tale entwined,
In sorrow's clasp, the heart confined.
A serenade for those who roam,
Guiding wayward spirits home.

The abyss cradles, dark yet fair,
With whispers floating through the air.
A ghostly lull, a gentle sigh,
Where echoes of the past still lie.

The Allure of Fathomless Pools

In shadows deep where secrets lie,
The gentle waves whisper and sigh.
Cascading dreams in azure hues,
Enchanting hearts with endless views.

Beneath the surface, magic brews,
With echoes of ancient, silent cues.
Glimmers dance in the water's embrace,
Nature's canvas, a wondrous space.

Adventure waits in the depths untamed,
Where each drop of water becomes unnamed.
In fathomless pools, the spirit glows,
Unveiling stories which the river knows.

The moonlight weaves a silvery thread,
Drawing the dreamers where lore is spread.
To plunge beneath in spirited flight,
Is to discover the hidden light.

With every ripple, the past awakes,
As currents pull, the heart often quakes.
For in the stillness, the allure remains,
Of fathomless pools where magic reigns.

Undercurrents of Past Lives

In the twilight hour, the waters speak,
Of tales forgotten, the brave and the weak.
Fragments of memories swirl in the tide,
Where shadows of history lovingly bide.

The pulse of time intertwines and bends,
As unseen forces, the river sends.
Each ripple a whisper, a story entwined,
Of lives once lived, and dreams defined.

Among the currents, the lost dreams rise,
With glimmers of hope and ancient sighs.
They linger like echoes, flickers of light,
Guiding the lost through the velvety night.

In depths of darkness, the truth takes form,
Underneath the surface, a powerful storm.
The past is alive, in shadows it thrives,
Through undulating waves, our spirit survives.

We drift on the lore that the water brings,
With hearts full of wonder, as the river sings.
The tapestry woven by time's gentle hand,
Invites us to dream, to understand.

Silent Ships Beneath the Moonlit Tide

Beneath the veil of the silver night,
Silent ships dance in ethereal light.
With sails unfurled like whispers untold,
They journey through waters where secrets unfold.

Each vessel a phantom, with stories to share,
Laden with memories afloat on the air.
They glide through dreams where the shadows sweep,
Guardians of sleep in the ocean deep.

With starlit heavens and gentle waves' sigh,
They navigate realms where time drifts by.
Beneath the calm, the heartbeats collide,
In silent ships, where dreams abide.

The moon casts its glow on the canvas of night,
Guiding the weary with tender light.
Sailing through whispers of ancient lore,
Awakening spirits to soar evermore.

Through silence profound, they search for a way,
To carry the dreams of the night into day.
The ships of the past in moonlit embrace,
Will carry our hopes, in time and in space.

Melodies of the Lurking Depths

From darkened waters where shadows glide,
Emerges a hymn from the ocean's side.
Melodies linger in the twilight's breath,
In harmony spun by the dance of death.

The depths resound with a haunting refrain,
Echoes of loss, laughter, and pain.
Each note a ripple, a touch on the soul,
Inviting the dreamers to lose control.

In the cradle of night, the tunes entwine,
Whispering tales like aged, mellowed wine.
With every ripple, new stories arise,
Carved by the stars in the endless skies.

The sirens call from the deep abyss,
With lullabies wrapped in starlit bliss.
A song that transcends the barrier of time,
Echoing softly, in silence, a chime.

For in the depths where the shadows creep,
The melodies of life secrets to keep.
In the swirling tides, beauty is found,
As the ocean croons its eternal sound.

Tidal Rhapsody of Untold Realms

In waves that dance with silver light,
The shadows play, a secret sight.
Where dreams are spun in salty air,
And whispered tales drift everywhere.

The sea's embrace, a timeless tune,
Beneath the gaze of the glowing moon.
With each surge, the stories soar,
Of hidden shores and ancient lore.

The currents weave a tapestry,
Of lands unseen, a mystery.
From depths profound, a voice does rise,
Echoing forth, through the endless skies.

When twilight falls and starlight gleams,
The ocean sings of forgotten dreams.
In salty mist, the echoes call,
A rhapsody, enchanting all.

So let us sail on tides of fate,
With hearts alive and spirits great.
For in the depth, we find our way,
In rapturous waves, we'll ever stay.

Ocean's Armory of Forgotten Echoes

Within the depths of azure gleam,
The ocean hides a silent dream.
An armory of tales untold,
In whispers soft, and mariner bold.

Each wave that crashes brings a sound,
Of treasures lost, on sunken ground.
A chorus of the deep rings clear,
Hints of the past, that linger near.

From coral reefs to shadowy caves,
The secrets swim in watery graves.
With every ebb, a story flows,
In currents where the wild wind blows.

The moonlight casts its silvery net,
As echoes of the past are met.
In whispered sighs of the briny air,
The ocean's armor holds its share.

So listen close; the sea imparts,
The echo of forgotten hearts.
In tides that turn, we find our place,
In the ocean's timeless embrace.

Paths Worn by Mystical Fins

Through waters deep where shadows dwell,
The mystical fins weave their spell.
In dance and play beneath the waves,
They guide the lost, the lonely braves.

With shimmering scales like shards of light,
They chase the sun, vanishing bright.
In paths unmarked by human hand,
They swim where the secrets of the sea stand.

Their laughter mingles with the breeze,
In azure depths, beneath the trees.
With every flick, they change the course,
Of currents strong with hidden force.

As moonlit trails unfold the night,
The whispers of fins ignite the light.
A journey shared through depths unknown,
By spirits of the sea, alone.

So follow where the waters lead,
To mystical realms where hearts are freed.
For in their path, the lost shall find,
The woven tales of love entwined.

A Murmuration of Feathery Algae

In currents warm where silence sways,
A murmuration softly plays.
With feathery algae, green and bright,
They twirl and dance in gentle light.

Like whispers shared 'neath water's veil,
In fluid grace, they weave a tale.
Of harmony, in ripples found,
In shimmering streams, where dreams abound.

As ocean currents weave their thread,
The algae flutter, quietly spread.
In patterns bold, their voices blend,
In nature's song that has no end.

Each drifting brush, a tale of old,
Of love's embrace in depths untold.
They paint the sea with emerald trails,
In secret worlds where beauty sails.

So let us linger by the shore,
Where murmurs call and spirits soar.
For in this dance of algae fine,
The ocean's heart, forever twines.

The Lost Songs of Drowned Stars

In depths where silence weeps,
The echoes of starlight fade.
Ghostly harmonies of the deep,
With time and tide they wade.

Melodies of forgotten nights,
Whispered in the ocean's breath.
Each note a flickering light,
Haunting tales of underwater death.

Once bright, now dim and far,
These voices dance in the brine.
They shimmer like a fallen star,
Trapped in the ebb of time.

Seafarers who seek their sound,
Might hear the songs they lost.
But in the waves, they are drowned,
Each voyage bears a cost.

So listen close when night is still,
For in the tide, they play.
The lost songs linger, yet they thrill,
Calling to the brave to stay.

Traces of Forgotten Tails

In shadows where the whispers dwell,
Forgotten tales weave through the sand.
Faint echoes of a carousel,
Of creatures lost, yet they stand.

With shimmering scales and fleeting grace,
Their stories linger in the light.
Each fin a ghost, each twist a trace,
Of vibrant worlds beyond our sight.

Tales of realms where dreams won't fade,
And laughter chases shadows near.
Where gentle hands of fate have played,
In realms where every secret's clear.

Yet time can dull the brightest hues,
And memories may slip away.
But still their essence we will choose,
In whispers of the ocean's sway.

So cast your nets and search the tide,
For forgotten tales await.
In every wave, their truths reside,
In currents that do not abate.

Reflections in Murky Waters

Beneath the surface, shadows creep,
Where light and darkness intertwine.
In murky depths, the secrets seep,
Like memories lost in the vine.

Reflections twist like fleeting dreams,
In liquid glass, they shimmer still.
Each ripple dances, or so it seems,
With whispers of the ocean's will.

A world obscured, yet deeply known,
With stories trapped in liquid gloom.
The beauty veiled, the truth unshown,
In depths where faded phantoms loom.

What lies beneath the water's skin,
A history worn like tattered lace?
Dive deep, tread soft, embrace the din,
And find your place in time's embrace.

So listen close to the silent thrall,
The murmurs of the waves will guide.
In every drop, in every call,
Are visions where the shadows bide.

Phantoms of the Metallic Reef

In realms where rust meets sapphire tide,
The phantoms frolic, slender and free.
Amongst the coral—colors collide,
In a dance of light, they breathe with glee.

A tapestry of sunken dreams,
Where treasures lay with stories old.
Each glinting shard of memory gleams,
As whispers share what's left untold.

They shimmer in shadows, wisps of grace,
Where steel meets sea and time suspends.
With every flicker, they trace their place,
In currents where reality bends.

So heed the tales of tides long passed,
The haunt of anchors, chains, and more.
For every phantom must hold fast,
To shipwrecked dreams on ocean's floor.

The metallic reef, a heart so bold,
In its embrace, the stories weave.
Through spectral dances, these dreams unfold,
In a world where we can still believe.

Fairytales from the Ocean Floor

In shadows deep where secrets lie,
The coral castles rise and sigh,
Whispers of mermaids, soft and bright,
Dance with the moonbeams in the night.

In tides that swirl with tales untold,
The silver fish in currents bold,
Sing of adventures, lost and found,
In the embrace of ocean's sound.

The octopus paints on sandy slate,
With brush of ink, it weaves fate,
Tangled in dreams of shimmering light,
Where spirit echoes through the night.

Through caverns dark, the sea will flow,
With treasures buried deep below,
And every shell a story holds,
Of fairytales in water's folds.

So dive beneath the azure hue,
Where magic breathes in shades of blue,
For in the depths, the heart shall soar,
To find those fairytales of yore.

The Fable of the Silken Sea

In waves like silk, the sea will sway,
A tapestry on light's ballet,
The sun will glisten, golden bright,
Weaving tales in soft twilight.

With every tide, a story spun,
Of daring quests 'neath setting sun,
Where sailors brave their hearts will lend,
To seek horizons without end.

A dolphin sings of dreams at play,
In playful arcs, they leap and sway,
While shadows dance on ocean's floor,
Whispers of fables that implore.

The winds will carry secrets far,
To distant shores where wishes are,
Each grain of sand, a promise sealed,
Of hope and love, forever healed.

So let the waves their songs extend,
To hearts entwined, to paths they send,
In every ripple, life anew,
A fable carved in ocean's blue.

Enchanted Ripples of Time

In gentle waves, the echoes play,
Revealing dreams of yesterday,
Where wishes dance on silver streams,
And weave the fabric of our dreams.

Each ripple holds a memory's gleam,
A fleeting thought, a whispered theme,
In twilight's hush, the heart will glow,
With tales that time will ever know.

The depths reveal a hidden lore,
Of lovers lost on distant shore,
As currents pull and winds do sigh,
Bound souls beneath the endless sky.

With every splash, a moment found,
In ocean's arms, we're gently bound,
To dance through realms of bright surprise,
A tapestry where magic lies.

So linger by the water's edge,
And heed the sea's enchanting pledge,
For in these ripples, time will blend,
Forever flows, with no end.

Siren's Gaze Over Sailor's Heart

Beneath the moon's seductive glow,
A siren waits with tides that flow,
Her haunting song calls out to thee,
In whispers soft, a melody.

With every note, a sailor's plight,
Drawn by her voice into the night,
His heart adrift, he sails afar,
To chase the dreams that leave a scar.

Upon the rocks, the waves will crash,
As fate entwines in a giddy flash,
Her gaze, a spell, that pulls him near,
A dance with danger, laced with fear.

Yet love can bloom where peril reigns,
In ocean's depths, where magic gains,
With every breath, a heartbeat lost,
In siren's song, he counts the cost.

So heed the winds and watch the sea,
For love and loss in harmony,
In every glance, a world apart,
The siren waits to steal his heart.

Ethereal Dances of the Deep

In shadowed realms where echoes play,
The sirens twirl in gleaming spray.
With whispers soft as mermaid's sigh,
They weave their spell beneath the sky.

Each ripple holds a tale untold,
Of treasures lost and legends bold.
The ocean's breath in gentle sways,
Moves through the night in mystic ways.

A silver fish, a fleeting glance,
Glides through the depths in liquid dance.
With every pulse, the currents hum,
An ancient song where dreams are spun.

In coral gardens, colors bloom,
The secret world beneath the gloom.
From tides that rise to ebbs that fall,
The deep reveals its siren call.

So come and lose your heart within,
Where mysteries of the deep begin.
With every wave, a memory bonds,
In ethereal dances of the beyond.

Luminous Secrets in Aquatic Currents

Beneath the waves, where light takes form,
The secrets swirl in a silent storm.
From pelagic depths to sandy shore,
The ocean hums of tales and more.

Glow of the jelly, ghostly and bright,
Guides the way through the darkest night.
With vibrant hues, they pulse and flare,
Alluring visions in salty air.

The whirls of water, a ballet divine,
Drawing you into their rhythmic line.
Each flicker hints at stories steeped,
In luminous depths where secrets keep.

A world unfolding, ethereal sights,
Where colors bloom and take to flights.
With each embrace of tide and swell,
The ocean's heart begins to tell.

So dive below, let wonder reign,
Among the secrets that ebb and wane.
In currents' hold, your spirit will glint,
In luminous waters, life's finest tint.

The Enigmatic Weaving of the Sea

Threads of water, ancient and wise,
Weave together 'neath endless skies.
In tapestry rich, the currents swirl,
As mysteries blend in a seamless whirl.

The kelp forests hide stories spun,
Of encounters made and battles won.
With dappled light filtering down,
Alluring secrets in the clowns.

Octopuses dance in a silent rhyme,
Crafting their tales through the sands of time.
With fluid grace, their stories flow,
In the enigmatic depths, we scarcely know.

A haunting call from the depths of blue,
Echoes of ages, old yet new.
From shipwrecked dreams to shimmering fate,
In woven depths, the tales await.

So linger long where the waters meet,
In a world where magic and wonder greet.
The sea unfolds its grand design,
In the enigmatic weaving, your heart will find.

Glistening Hues in the Depth's Caress

Beneath the surface, colors play,
In vibrant dance, the sea's ballet.
A canvas rich with shades untold,
Where glistening hues in currents fold.

By sunlit rays and moon's embrace,
The ocean crafts a jeweled lace.
Each wave a brush, each splash a note,
In harmony, the waters float.

Coral kingdoms, a rich array,
Dwell in shadows where kelpies sway.
With every flicker, light draws near,
As tranquil depths shed their bright veneer.

So dive into this world of gloss,
Where mystic shadows weave their toss.
With every glance, a treasure dressed,
In glistening hues, the sea's caress.

So linger long and drift away,
In dancing tides where wonders play.
For in the depths, you'll surely find,
A vibrant heart that knows no bind.

Tales from the Coral Castle

In the depths where colors swirl,
A castle stands, a hidden pearl.
With seaweed tapestries and shells so bright,
Guardians of dreams in the moon's soft light.

Mermaids sing with voices clear,
Echoing softly for those who hear.
They weave their stories in the tide,
Where magic and mystery, they don't hide.

The dolphins dance beneath the waves,
In secret paths where the ocean saves.
With laughter that sparkles like the sun,
In coral halls where tales are spun.

Fishes wink in the twilight glow,
In coral mazes, through currents they flow.
Each creature a player in this grand play,
Their secrets hidden from light of day.

So listen close to the ocean's song,
Where tales are whispered, and dreams belong.
In the coral castle, life takes flight,
In the depths, where day meets night.

A Symphony Undersea

Beneath the waves, a tune begins,
A symphony played where the ocean spins.
The sea's soft heart beats in time,
With melodies rich, and rhythms sublime.

The starfish sway to a gentle beat,
While sea turtles move with grace and heat.
A concert for creatures both big and small,
In the aquatic hall where the echoes call.

The conch shells sing with a haunting sound,
While coral trumpets grow all around.
An orchestra formed of currents and light,
In the depths, when day fades to night.

Seahorses twirl in a lovely dance,
In a ballet of bubbles, they take a chance.
With each flick of fin, a story unfolds,
In the symphony where magic beholds.

So dive down deep and lend an ear,
To the symphony that all creatures hear.
In the heart of the blue, let your dreams flow,
In the music of waves, let your spirit grow.

Fantasy Bubbles in the Shoreline Night

Under the stars, where shadows play,
Bubbles of dreams float softly away.
In the soft sand, stories lie,
Waiting for whispers to breathe and fly.

Crabs in armor scuttle about,
While the moon weaves magic, there's no doubt.
Each wave that crashes on the shore,
Sings of adventures, and even more.

A lighthouse stands with its guiding light,
Illuminating wonders in the night.
With every splash, a fantasy grows,
In the shimmering sea, where anything goes.

Starfish twinkle with secrets bright,
In the embrace of water, under the light.
With wishes trapped in bubbles' embrace,
The shoreline reveals a hidden place.

So wander the sand, let your heart soar,
Through bubbles of dreams, through the ocean's door.
In this shoreline night, let your spirit ignite,
Against the vast canvas of heavenly night.

Watercolors of the Ocean's Heart

With a brush of waves, the ocean paints,
Watercolors swirl with colors faint.
The deep calls out in shades so bright,
A canvas alive in the warm sunlight.

Greens and blues, a dazzling array,
Flow like whispers where sea creatures play.
Each stroke of tide tells a tale anew,
In the heart of the sea, where dreams are true.

Goldfish glide like strokes of the sun,
In the artwork of life, we all are one.
With barnacles clinging in ruffled dress,
The ocean's heart beats with nothing less.

Shells, like palettes, scatter the shore,
Each holding secrets of legends and lore.
In this gallery of life, we drift and sway,
In the watercolors of another day.

So come, behold this vibrant sight,
In the ocean's art, find your delight.
For in each wave and each gentle part,
Lies the essence of the ocean's heart.

Whirlpools of Forgotten Legends

In the depths where shadows weave,
Whispers echo, tales they leave.
Heroes lost and battles fought,
Secrets hidden, battles sought.

Stars align in darkened skies,
Brave the hearts that dare to rise.
Spirits dance in waters deep,
Guardians the ancient keep.

A swirling fate, a fateful dream,
In this realm, more than it seems.
Time forgets the lives they led,
Yet their legends linger, unsaid.

Runes inscribed on weathered stone,
Echoes of a time long known.
Adventure waits in ebb and flow,
Where the bravest dare to go.

Whirlpools churn with heart and lore,
Carrying tales from distant shore.
In their depths, gold waits to find,
A map to realms of the timeless kind.

Delicate Filaments in the Coral Garden

Beneath the waves, a world so bright,
Coral castles in morning light.
Delicate threads of crimson and gold,
Whispering stories of nature bold.

Gentle creatures weave in and out,
In this realm without a doubt.
Each flicker tells a tale of grace,
Nature's dance in a vibrant place.

The ocean's breath a soothing song,
Its rhythms where we all belong.
Sheltered by the corals' bloom,
Life thrives beneath, no fear of gloom.

Kaleidoscope of hues and dreams,
Dancing light in sparkling streams.
Here, the heart finds peace anew,
In the shades of turquoise blue.

Threads of magic, soft and fine,
Entwined like fate, a sacred line.
In the currents, stories gather,
In the depths, a timeless lover.

Tales of Driftwood and Moonlit Waves

Moonlight drapes the silver sea,
Tales of driftwood, wild and free.
Each piece a story yet untold,
Whispers of journeys, brave and bold.

Resting softly on the shore,
Echoes linger, longing for more.
Through the nights of tempest and tears,
Fables crafted through the years.

The waves lap gently, softening time,
Each rhythmic pulse a whispered rhyme.
Seagulls circle, a spirited song,
Nature's chorus, profound and strong.

With every tide, new dreams arise,
In the foam where the secret lies.
Driftwood speaks in its own way,
Guiding hearts that choose to stay.

Underneath the celestial glow,
Adventures beckon, tides will flow.
As night unfolds its velvet shroud,
The ocean whispers, wild and proud.

Veils of Mist on the Tidal Edge

Veils of mist weave tales so grey,
In the early light of day.
Tidal whispers, secrets float,
Echoes soft, a ghostly note.

The shore holds memories of the tide,
Where hearts once danced, now they bide.
Footprints lost in shifting sands,
Tracing paths of ancient hands.

Time unfolds like morning dew,
In a world both fresh and new.
Glimmers of a distant land,
Stories told, together we stand.

Watch the waves as they play and tease,
With haunting sighs and gentle ease.
In the mist, the heart will see,
Ghostly figures, wild and free.

Veils of time, a soft embrace,
Carrying whispers through this space.
Drawn together by the sea,
Bound by stories, you and me.

The Perilous Beauty of Seashell Halls

In halls where seashells glimmer bright,
Tales untold come to light.
Whispers of waves from far-off shores,
In the quiet, adventure roars.

With every seashell, a story swells,
Of maiden's charms and ocean spells.
Softly in the moon's embrace,
Secrets of the deep we trace.

Among the coral and the sand,
Echoes of a longing strand.
Curled dreams that drift with the tide,
In these halls where wonders hide.

Glistening pearls and starfish' grace,
Navigating time and space.
With every tide that ebbs and flows,
The perilous beauty forever glows.

A symphony of colors bold,
In visions deep and stories told.
Among the shells, we seek and find,
The pulse of oceans intertwined.

Harmonics of the Tidal Dance

Beneath the moon's soft silver hue,
The tides compose their haunting tune.
A dance of waves, both fierce and frail,
In rhythmic whispers, secrets sail.

With every rush, the sea's embrace,
A timeless song through endless space.
Where echoes of an ancient lore,
Resound upon the sandy shore.

In swirling currents, dreams arise,
Reflecting stars in starlit skies.
The harmonics of this wild delight,
Bring the fallen night to light.

Water's caress upon the stone,
In twilight's glow, we find our home.
A melody of ebb and flow,
The tidal dance forever grows.

Feel the beat of nature's heart,
As worlds within the ocean start.
With wave and wind, we rise and fall,
In perfect harmony, we call.

Fables of the Emerald Expanses

In emerald depths, the fables dwell,
Of creatures wise, with tales to tell.
With glistening scales that catch the eye,
In swirling currents, secrets lie.

Elders whisper of lost delights,
In the glow of phosphorescent nights.
Beneath the surface, wonders gleam,
As dreamers long for the whispers' theme.

From coral reefs to gentle bays,
In vivid hues, the ocean sways.
Guardians of the hidden lore,
In every wave, a tale to explore.

The laughter of a dolphin's grace,
A voyage through this sacred space.
Each ripple carries whispers clear,
Of fables floating ever near.

Turn the page, and you will see,
The emerald expanses set us free.
With hearts ablaze and spirits bold,
In ocean's fables, life unfolds.

Nostalgia of the Sunken Dreams

Beneath the waves where memories sleep,
The sunken dreams in silence seep.
Fragments of time, like grains of sand,
In faded whispers, futures planned.

Echos of laughter, the sailor's plight,
Chasing the dawn, embracing night.
Where ships once sailed on voyage grand,
Now lie dormant on the ocean's hand.

Ghosts of wishes drift in the deep,
In currents strong, their secrets keep.
A realm of shadows and ancient stones,
Where nostalgia breathes in whispered tones.

Flickers of hope in depths untold,
A tapestry in blue and gold.
Remembered faces fade away,
Yet linger softly in the spray.

In the realm where dreams intertwine,
The sunken past feels so divine.
With every wave, a tale reborn,
In ocean's heart, our souls adorn.

Abyssal Melodies in Forgotten Tides

In the depths where whispers dwell,
Echoes dance with silent bells.
Shadows sway in liquid grace,
Secrets drift in time and space.

Bubbles rise like fleeting dreams,
Carried forth on starlit streams.
Crabs compose a symphony,
In a realm behind the sea.

Tides tell tales of ancient lore,
Of shipwrecks and forgotten shore.
Moonlight spills on coral beds,
Where the ocean's magic spreads.

Faint refrains of ocean's plight,
Guide lost hearts through endless night.
Serpentine the waves do weave,
As the world below believes.

Melodies in currents glide,
In twilight's grasp they quietly bide.
Listen close, the water's song,
In every note, you'll find where you belong.

The Chords of the Submerged Realm

Beneath the depths where silence reigns,
Echos pulse in watery veins.
Anemones sway with gentle might,
In the twilight of fading light.

Starfish scribe their stories old,
In shimmering tales of vibrant gold.
Octopuses spin their mystic dance,
Caught in a fluid, cosmic trance.

Currents weave through rocky seams,
Stirring up forgotten dreams.
With each wave a memory stirs,
Amongst the whispers, time occurs.

The sea anemone softly glows,
An orchestra where no one knows.
Crashing sounds and tranquil sighs,
Compose a song beneath the skies.

Bubbles rise, a sharp intake,
Reminding us of how hearts ache.
In the tide, we seek and find,
The rhythms of our hearts combined.

Whimsical Encounters in Ocean's Gaps

In hidden coves, where secrets scheme,
Ocean critters laugh and dream.
Seahorses twirl in playful spin,
Whispering tales of where they've been.

Schools of fish in colors bright,
Dance beneath the fading light.
Each fin flicks in lively jest,
While the stingrays glide with zest.

Mermaids hide in velvet tides,
With laughter where the sea resides.
Their melodies draw one to roam,
In the solace of their home.

Starry skies, the waves do kiss,
Each embrace a transient bliss.
With seashells singing soft refrains,
In the chorus of ocean's chains.

Whimsical jests in salty air,
Lead us forth without a care.
Beyond the horizon's gleaming line,
Where fantasy and truth entwine.

Journey Through the Waving Grass

Through verdant fields where breezes sway,
The grass whispers secrets of the day.
In emerald waves, we laugh and run,
Chasing shadows, chasing sun.

Butterflies weave in patterns bright,
A ballet of colors, sheer delight.
Each petal, a note in nature's song,
In this moment, we all belong.

The whispers of leaves tell tales of old,
Of summer's warmth and winters cold.
Every blade a story holds,
In the tapestry of life, unfolds.

Stars peek out as daylight fades,
Casting spells through silvery glades.
Underneath the twilight's gaze,
We find magic in a gentle maze.

Hand in hand, we wander wide,
Through fields where dreams and hopes collide.
In the wave of grass, we discover,
The endless journey of one another.

Whirling Mystique of Salty Air

Upon the breeze, whispers soar,
Secrets kept on the ocean's floor.
With each gust, a tale untold,
Of dreams and wishes brightly bold.

Seagulls dance in a swirling flight,
Guiding hearts towards day and night.
Salt-shined treasures glimmer fair,
Calling forth the whirling air.

Misty cliffs hold stories wide,
Of sailors lost in the turning tide.
Ancient mariners, fears to share,
In the haunting depths, we find despair.

Underneath the moon's soft sway,
The waves that sigh, they craft their play.
In the twilight's gentle dare,
Echoes linger through the air.

With laughter bright, the stars align,
Hints of magic blend, divine.
The salty breeze, a loving care,
Wraps us close in whispers rare.

Threads of Myth Beneath the Foam

In the depths where shadows dwell,
Memories weave a hidden spell.
Threads of gold and silver shine,
Beneath the waves, a tale divine.

Mermaids sing in haunting grace,
Calling forth the heart's embrace.
Every ripple, every foam,
Holds a myth that feels like home.

Treasures lost and battles fought,
In the ocean's grasp, wisdom sought.
Ancient echoes drift and roam,
Binding souls to tales of foam.

Fishermen tell of sights unseen,
Wonders lurk in waters green.
Nets cast wide, the secrets roam,
Threads of myth in every comb.

In the depths where dreams unite,
Revelations shine so bright.
Underneath the seaborne dome,
Life's secrets spin from foam to foam.

Echos from Shattered Conch Shelters

Upon the shore, where shells lie broken,
Lives the silence of words unspoken.
In conch shelters, stories blend,
Of ocean's joy and timeless end.

Whispers drift on the salt-kissed air,
Hints of lives that flourished rare.
Shattered walls hold echoes clear,
Of laughter, love, and fleeting fear.

The tides will wash away their plight,
Leaving traces of fading light.
In every crack, a tale of woe,
Echos dance as waters flow.

Sun-kissed sands where memories dwell,
Each conch shell holds a secret spell.
With every wave, a voice will call,
From shattered homes where shadows fall.

In the hush of twilight's glow,
These fragments sing of long ago.
A symphony of where we've been,
In shattered conchs, our lives begin.

The Allure of Enchanted Waters

Beneath the waves, a vibrant hue,
The allure that shines in every view.
Where mermaids play and sirens sing,
Enchanted waters hold their spring.

Reflections dance on the cool blue tide,
Magic flows with every glide.
In hidden caves, where secrets dwell,
The depths allure, cast a spell.

Waves embrace the sunlit shore,
Whispering tales forevermore.
In their grasp, the strong and meek,
The allure of waters, soft yet sleek.

Every splash tells a story bright,
Of ships that sail into the night.
The ocean's heart, wild and free,
Calls to dreamers, come and see.

Within each wave, an echo lies,
Of dreams that pierce the vast, blue skies.
In enchanted waters, hearts will soar,
Forever bound to the ocean's lore.

Legends of the Siren's Lament

In twilight's glow, the siren sings,
Her voice a whisper through the wings.
A haunting tale where shadows dwell,
Beneath the waves, a longing swell.

Her beauty lures the sailors near,
Yet echoes drown in salty fear.
For every heart that comes to roam,
Is swallowed by the ocean's foam.

With shimmering scales and eyes like stars,
She weaves her spells from afar.
A melody of love and loss,
In currents deep, they pay the cost.

Her tears fall soft, like silver rain,
Each drop a note, a whispered pain.
For every soul she guides amiss,
The ocean holds her bittersweet kiss.

In legends told 'neath moonlit skies,
The siren's song forever flies.
A tale of choice, of fate entwined,
In waters dark, the heart's resigned.

Veils of the Ocean's Enchantment

Beneath the froth, a secret lies,
In shadows deep, the magic sighs.
Veils of mist where spirits weave,
An ancient dance the waters cleave.

Waves that shimmer, blue and bright,
Hold echoes of the starry night.
With every ripple, stories flow,
Of dreams and wishes long ago.

Sirens hum their ghostly tune,
Beneath the silver, watch the moon.
In the depths where silence reigns,
The ocean holds her deep refrains.

Mariners whisper, hearts in thrall,
To ocean's call, they rise and fall.
Each echo carries tales entwined,
In veils of blue, lost hopes confined.

So listen well, when waves arise,
For ocean's heart knows no goodbyes.
In veils of magic, soul takes flight,
A realm where day meets endless night.

Currents of Dreaming Waters

In dreaming waters, secrets swirl,
As moonlight casts its silken pearl.
The currents hum a lullaby,
Where time stands still and spirits fly.

Beneath the surface, visions glide,
In tranquil tides, where dreams abide.
With every splash, a wish takes form,
In sacred flow, the heart feels warm.

The depths resonate with stories spun,
As shadows dance, and fates are won.
Whispers brush the ocean's skin,
In every wave, a tale begins.

As starlit skies above reflect,
The waters sing of hopes unchecked.
In currents strong, each dreamers sails,
Find shelter in the moonlit trails.

So drift awhile in dreaming's grace,
Let waters lead you to that place.
Where hearts will mend, and spirits soar,
In currents deep, forevermore.

The Glistening Depths of Solitude

In shimmering depths, where shadows fade,
Solitude hums its quiet serenade.
The ocean cradles broken dreams,
In silence wrapped, its stillness beams.

Each wave a sigh, each tide a tear,
Embracing whispers of those held dear.
For in the heart of waters wide,
Lies solace sought, and hope denied.

With every drift, a story told,
The depths conceal both young and old.
A hidden world, where echoes dwell,
In glistening pools, a haunting spell.

The solitude, a gentle friend,
In ocean's arms, we find our end.
To linger here, where silence keeps,
A treasure trove, where memory sleeps.

So let the waves your worries fold,
In glistening depths, true peace behold.
With every ebb, let kindness flow,
In solitude's embrace, we grow.

Secrets Beneath Silver Waves

In twilight's glow, they shimmer bright,
The secrets sunk in waters tight.
Echoes whisper from depths unknown,
Tales of old in currents flown.

Mermaids sigh with gentle grace,
Their laughter lingers, leaves a trace.
Bubbles rise with ancient lore,
Beneath the waves, forevermore.

Moonlight dances on the sea,
Each silver wave a mystery.
With every crest, the stories weave,
Hints of magic, if you believe.

The tide reveals what dusk conceals,
A world alive, where nature heals.
In whispered tones, the ocean speaks,
Of treasure found in hidden creeks.

A treasure map of starlit dreams,
Written in the sea's quiet schemes.
Dive with courage, chase the flow,
For in its depths, true wonders glow.

The Lullaby of Distant Shores

In the hush of night unspun,
Soft melodies, a tale begun.
The waves hum low, a lullaby,
To cradle hearts that drift and sigh.

Stars twinkle in a velvet sky,
While breezes weave a gentle sigh.
Each breath of wind, a soothing balm,
Where echoes chant, the world is calm.

From distant lands, the whispers call,
Of splendor found beyond the wall.
Sailing forth on dreams untold,
With starlight guiding, brave and bold.

Footprints trace on sandy floors,
As night unveils its secret doors.
The sea, a cradle, rocking slow,
In twilight's arms, our spirits flow.

Embrace the night, let shadows glide,
Where wishes float on every tide.
For in this lullaby so sweet,
The heart finds peace, and time's retreat.

Tides Turned by Silent Melodies

As twilight wakes, the sea reveals,
A symphony that gently steals.
Soft notes that drift on evening air,
Compose a magic, light and rare.

Currents hum a ballad clear,
Inviting dreams that wander near.
With every wave, the music swells,
In hidden depths where mystery dwells.

The ocean plays a timeless song,
Its rhythm deep, where hearts belong.
Listen close, let silence reign,
For in the stillness, joy is gained.

The tides respond to silent sound,
In movements lost, the world is found.
Through whispered chants of night's embrace,
We find our place, a sacred space.

Let melodies of water weave,
A tapestry we can believe.
For in the craft of nature's tune,
We dance beneath the silver moon.

A Dance in Celestial Currents

Beneath the stars, the waters spin,
A cosmic waltz, where dreams begin.
Galaxies glimmer, an astral stage,
As tides sway softly, page by page.

Waves like ribbons, twirling bright,
Whisper secrets to the night.
In every splash, the universe sings,
While moonlit beams dance on silken wings.

Celestial currents draw us near,
As stardust drips in the atmosphere.
Hearts entwined in the ocean's arms,
Feel the pulse of timeless charms.

With every crest, we leap and spin,
Under the gaze of stars within.
Tangled dreams in a cosmic flow,
Where love ignites and spirits glow.

Come, take my hand, let's sway and glide,
In this ballet the stars provide.
Together, we'll meet the sky's embrace,
In the currents of time, we'll find our place.

Tangles of Dream and Tide

In whispered winds, the night unfolds,
A tapestry of stars in gold.
Upon the shore, where dreams collide,
The ebbing whispers of the tide.

With every wave, a secret spun,
A tale of moon and warmth of sun.
They dance like echoes in the night,
A fleeting glimpse of pure delight.

O, dreams entwined in salty air,
A world where hopes are light as air.
With every crest, a wish takes flight,
To chase the shadows of the night.

In corners where the currents flow,
A labyrinth of thoughts we sow.
We wander through the deep unknown,
In tangles where our hearts have grown.

And as the stars begin to fade,
We find the paths the fates have laid.
In every splash, a story blooms,
In salty depths, our spirit grooms.

Lure of the Ocean's Embrace

The ocean whispers tales of old,
Of distant shores and riches bold.
In every wave, a song unique,
A siren's call, a lover's peek.

Beneath the moonglow's gentle kiss,
Lies a world wrapped in sweet bliss.
With arms outstretched, the sea invites,
To dance with shadows, day and nights.

The foam that frolics on the sand,
Paints dreams with a graceful hand.
With currents strong, it draws us near,
A melody we long to hear.

In swirling tides, there's magic spun,
In every heart, the ocean's fun.
A lure that pulls from depths unknown,
A chance to claim what's never shown.

And as the dawn reveals her face,
We find ourselves in the ocean's grace.
In every crest, a parting gift,
A promise made, a spirit's lift.

Fantasies in the Aquatic Realm

Beneath the waves, where secrets sigh,
The dreams of ancients softly lie.
With colors bright like liquid light,
They lure the heart, igniting flight.

In coral castles, stories weave,
Of whispered wishes, dreams believe.
Each ripple forms a tale anew,
In spiral dances, life's debut.

The playful dolphins leap and twirl,
In liquid realms where wonders swirl.
Their laughter echoes, free and wild,
A serenade of nature's child.

The shimmering fish, a vivid hue,
Painting the waters in shades so true.
They beckon souls to dive inside,
To chase the currents, to abide.

With every splash, a tale takes flight,
In fantasies that thrill the night.
The ocean's heart, a boundless dream,
In its embrace, we find our theme.

Shadows of the Wistful Sea

In twilight's breath, the sea reveals,
A canvas washed in wistful feels.
With shadows deep, and whispers low,
The secrets of the tides bestow.

Where moonlight dances on the waves,
Lies all the stories of the braves.
In every splash, a memory wakes,
A journey forged through time's own lakes.

The gentle breeze pulls at our dreams,
As we traverse these silver beams.
In every curl of salted spray,
The past emerges, here to stay.

And through the mist, a vision gleams,
Of starlit paths and hopeful schemes.
In shadows cast by evening's grace,
We wander on this timeless space.

As day surrenders to the night,
The sea unveils her quiet light.
In wistful tones, our hearts align,
With shadows of the sea divine.

Whispers of the Ocean's Braid

In the deep, where secrets weave,
The tides hum songs, so hard to believe.
Whispers drift on the salty air,
Calling the lost with tender care.

Moonlit dance of shimmering spray,
Guides the wanderer, night or day.
Echoes pulse through shells and sand,
Crafting stories that will withstand.

Currents swirl with ancient grace,
Every stroke, a lover's embrace.
In every wave, a tale unfolds,
Adventures waiting to be told.

Stars aligned on ocean's breast,
Signs of journeys, dreams expressed.
With the dawn, the world awakes,
As the ocean's breath softly shakes.

Beneath the foam, the treasures lie,
Guarded by the restless sky.
Listen close, and you will find,
The ocean's heart is intertwined.

Shimmering Tendrils of Distant Shores

From horizon's edge, a shimmer glows,
Distant whispers, the ocean knows.
Tendrils reach like a lover's hand,
Inviting all to its enchanted land.

Golden sands and azure dreams,
Where sunlight dances, and magic gleams.
Every grain a story spun,
Of battles fought and victories won.

Beneath the waves, a world unfolds,
Where mermaids sing and magic holds.
Coral castles nestled tight,
Cradled in the arms of night.

The gentle pulse of tides in flow,
Washes away the pain and woe.
With each crest, a new beginning,
Life's grand play, eternally spinning.

In twilight's embrace, the echoes rise,
A serenade beneath the skies.
Heartbeats mix with ocean's roar,
An endless dance on a timeless shore.

Secrets of the Salty Veil

Behind the waves, where shadows drift,
Salty secrets, the ocean's gift.
Veils of spray guard what lies below,
Mysteries whispered in tides that flow.

Sunlight dappled on rolling tide,
Hides the dreams that diverge and collide.
Each crest carries a ship's last sigh,
Resting beneath the azure sky.

Crabs scuttle and fish dart near,
In the ocean's heart, there's nothing to fear.
Hidden treasures beckon still,
Beyond the shore, beyond the thrill.

Each drop of salt, each grain of sand,
Is woven tightly in sea's command.
Listen closely, the tales will bloom,
Of distant lands and impending doom.

With every gale, a new refrain,
A symphony of loss and gain.
The salty veil pulls tightly down,
Into the depths, where dreams are drowned.

Lace of the Abyssal Dream

In the depth of night, the waters sigh,
A lace of dreams that floats nearby.
Tangled thoughts in currents weave,
Secrets buried, hard to believe.

Eerie lights in shadowed swirls,
Guide lost souls and drifting pearls.
Every whisper hints at truth,
Promises made in the bloom of youth.

Silent echoes, so soft and deep,
Guard the stories the ocean keeps.
Eyes like currents, endless and vast,
Holding memories of the past.

When the moon spills silver on the tide,
The abyss reveals what we often hide.
Fingers trace the lace of night,
A ballet of shadows, dim yet bright.

Remember well, the ocean's song,
In every moment, you belong.
Tied to dreams that swirl and gleam,
In the heart of the abyssal dream.

Trident of Dusk and Dawn

In shadow's grasp, the trident gleams,
A whispering wind, where magic dreams.
Beneath the sky, in twilight's embrace,
It charts the waves, a silent grace.

With each stroke, the colors blend,
As day and night in silence mend.
The sea holds tales of old and grand,
Awake the legends, seashells in hand.

In depths unseen, where secrets sleep,
The tides will rise, the currents sweep.
A dance of stars, a shimmering glow,
On dusky paths where wishes flow.

Fear not the storms that brew and roar,
For with each crash, there's something more.
The trident sings, a lullaby,
To hearts that dare to roam and fly.

So hold it firm, this mythic spear,
And wander forth, without a fear.
For dusk and dawn reside in you,
Embrace their power, brave and true.

Twilight Meet on Salty Shores

Where ocean meets the hidden light,
The twilight whispers, taking flight.
On salty shores, the dreams arise,
As stars awaken in velvet skies.

The waves, they speak in softest tones,
A serenade, where magic's sown.
With every crash, the secrets spill,
Of treasure lost and dreams to fill.

A breeze carries tales of old,
Of sailors brave and countless gold.
In the air, a shimmer gleams,
Like echoes lost in distant dreams.

The moonlight dances on the tide,
As shadows weave, their fate they bide.
With each embrace, the world stands still,
While hearts entwine with magic's thrill.

So linger here, where time suspends,
On salty shores, where love transcends.
For in this twilight's tender glow,
The soul finds peace, as rivers flow.

Fen of the Mystical Angler

In marshy realms, where mist prevails,
The angler's song on breezes sails.
A gentle cast beneath the boughs,
Where ancient trees and secrets rouse.

The water ripples, tales untold,
Of fish that shimmer in hues of gold.
With baited breath, the patient waits,
As dreams emerge at twilight's gates.

Each flick and splash, a whisper shared,
In every cast, the heart laid bare.
With nets of hope and lines of trust,
The fen unfolds its treasures, just.

Amid the reeds where shadows blend,
And moonlit whispers softly wend.
The mystical frog croaks ancient lore,
Of those who dared to seek and explore.

So heed the call of tales that leap,
Where waters watch, and secrets keep.
In fen's embrace, let spirits soar,
To find the magic you search for.

The Radiance of Siren's Secrets

Beneath the waves where sirens sing,
A melody of forgotten things.
In crystal depths, their voices flow,
A calling deep, where heartbeats glow.

With every note, the sea inspires,
Filling the night with ancient fires.
Their secrets weave through currents strong,
A timeless tale, both right and wrong.

Lured by beauty, sailors stray,
In shimmering light, they lose their way.
Yet in their eyes, the love remains,
Reflections forged through joy and pains.

The tide holds wisdom, deep and vast,
A siren's song, relentless, cast.
For those who dare to pause and hear,
The ocean's heart beats loud and clear.

So linger by the jagged shores,
Let waves reveal their hidden scores.
For in the radiance, seeks your soul,
The siren's secrets make you whole.

The Haunting Siren's Echo

In shadows cast by moonlit glow,
Whispers ride the waves below.
A melody that cuts the night,
Echoing dreams of ghostly flight.

Hearts entwined with longing's song,
Call from depths, where souls belong.
A haunting tune lures sailors near,
To secrets hidden, wrapped in fear.

Lurking dangers swirl and creep,
As silence wraps the sea in sleep.
Yet still the siren's voice will rise,
A spell woven 'neath stormy skies.

Her song of magic, loss, and woe,
Guides the ships to where they go.
And with each wave, the tale unfurls,
Of fateful love in twisting swirls.

But heed the warning, seek the light,
For shadows blend with endless night.
In every note, a curse is spun,
By the haunting echo, all hope undone.

Murmurs of the Depths' Lullaby

Beneath the waves, where silence grows,
A lullaby of water flows.
Cradled in the sea's embrace,
Whispers of time and endless space.

The gentle waves, like hands so soft,
Lift weary hearts and spirits aloft.
In the current, dreams take flight,
Dancing freely in the night.

As currents pull, a story spins,
Of ancient tales where life begins.
Embers of hope in the foam aglow,
Murmurs of depths, forever flow.

In the ocean's grasp, a song will swell,
Siren-like, it casts its spell.
With every note, a promise made,
In the depths where dreams won't fade.

Listen close to the secrets shared,
In the waters where souls are bared.
A lullaby that knows no end,
Through thundering waves, the heart will mend.

Gossamer Dreams on a Seafoam Breeze

On gossamer wings, the dreams take flight,
Carried forth on winds of night.
The seafoam kisses the sandy shore,
Whispers of legends and so much more.

In twilight's glow, fantasies bloom,
Bathing the world in silvered gloom.
Echoes of laughter, soft and warm,
In the embrace of the ocean's charm.

Glittering stars mirror the waves,
As mysteries sway in watery graves.
Hope floats lightly, a feather's grace,
In the arms of the sea, our sacred place.

Sails unfurled to the open air,
Guided by a feeling rare.
And in each breath, the promise we seize,
Of gossamer dreams on a seafoam breeze.

So drift away on this gentle tide,
Let imagination be your guide.
For in each wave, a story is spun,
Of whispered dreams and nights begun.

Mysteries Entwined in Saltwater Whirls

In tangled threads of currents deep,
Lie secrets that the oceans keep.
Saltwater whirls, a dance of fate,
Where time stands still, and hearts palpitate.

Underneath, a world untamed,
A symphony of life unnamed.
Creatures linger, shadows play,
In the depths, lost tales lay.

Each swirl conceals a story bold,
Of ancient mariners and treasures told.
As the tide turns, a new path clears,
To uncover hopes, to banish fears.

Mysteries rise in watery glow,
Entwined with fears that we all know.
And with the dawn, the sun will shine,
On secrets held by the brine.

So dive deep into waters wide,
Let your spirit be your guide.
For in each swirl, a fragment sways,
Of mysteries lost in ocean's maze.

Mysteries of the Enchanted Abyss

In shadows deep, the secrets dwell,
Where whispers ride on ocean's swell.
A labyrinth of dreams and fears,
Beneath the waves, the truth appears.

The siren's song, a haunting tune,
Beneath the watchful gaze of moon.
With every pulse, the waters sigh,
A timeless dance as spirits fly.

Lost treasures in the midnight blue,
Ancient tales that brush anew.
Through the depths where darkness weaves,
A world unlocked beyond the leaves.

In silent depths, the ancients play,
Guarding secrets from the day.
An endless quest, a heart's allure,
In boundless waves forever pure.

Glimmers fade as shadows blend,
In the abyss, all things transcend.
With every tide, a moment fades,
The mysteries dance in twilight glades.

Whispers of the Coral Veil

Through coral gardens, whispers drift,
In colors bright, the waters lift.
A gentle dance, a secret cheer,
Where dreams of ocean's heart draw near.

Beneath the surface, stories old,
Of brave explorers, tales bold.
The flicker of fins in twilight's glow,
Hides treasures only mermaids know.

With every wave, the sea does speak,
A tongue of magic, soft yet sleek.
In vibrant hues, life's wonders beam,
Tangled in the ocean's dream.

Songs of shells against the tide,
Gifts of the sea, our hearts confide.
In gentle currents, laughter weaves,
Through coral veils where the heart believes.

Underneath the azure sky,
The spirit of the ocean sighs.
With every ripple, stories twine,
In the whispers of the coral line.

Echoes of Untamed Tides

In tumult's grip, the waters churn,
A tempest's roar, the pages turn.
With every wave that breaks ashore,
Whispers linger, tales of yore.

Those winds that howl through weary sails,
Carry dreams of ancient tales.
In the echoes, spirits rise,
From depths unseen, they draw their guise.

The perilous dance, the thrill of flight,
As stars emerge to greet the night.
With tides that pulse and swell with might,
The wild sea claims her rightful right.

Through storms that brew, our hearts align,
As echoes call, and stars entwine.
In restless seas, our fates arise,
The untamed tides, beneath the skies.

From quiet shores to raging foam,
In each wave, a heart finds home.
The ocean's call, forever bright,
In echoes deep, our spirits light.

Secrets in the Seafoam Shadows

In twinkling light, where shadows blend,
The sea's soft lap, a whispered friend.
In secrets held within the brine,
The stories weave a path divine.

Ghostly forms in seafoam dance,
A fleeting glimpse, a daring chance.
Through delicate threads of twilight sheen,
The mysteries linger, soft and keen.

With secrets laced in salt and spray,
The ocean's heart will lead the way.
In every crest, in every fall,
A tapestry of dreams to call.

Beneath the waves, where shadows thrive,
The pulse of time, the will to strive.
An ancient song, forever flows,
Within the seafoam, magic grows.

In the depths where shadows play,
The secrets of the sea convey.
With every wave, the world reclaims,
The whispers held in ocean's names.

Starlit Conversations with the Sea

Under the moon's soft embrace,
The tides whisper secrets untold,
Waves dance with a delicate grace,
Their stories of sailors, brave and bold.

Shells glimmer like stars on the shore,
As shadows of night drape the land,
The ocean's heart beats evermore,
In the language of both sea and sand.

Voices of mermaids float on high,
Carrying laughter in salty air,
While echoes of ships drift and sigh,
In the depths where dreams find their lair.

Each ripple a note in the song,
Where time loses all of its weight,
And every heartbeat feels like a throng,
Of wonders that wait at the gate.

So come, dear friend, to the tide's call,
Let starlit paths guide our way,
For in the hush of night, we shall fall,
Into the sea's captivating play.

The Enigma of Waving Shallows

Beneath the waves, a secret unfolds,
In the shimmering dance of light,
What mysteries do the shallows hold?
A world concealed, veiled from sight.

The whispering reeds, the gurgling stream,
Crabs scuttle briskly, shadows parade,
In sunlit depths, a lingering dream,
Of adventure and riddles that fade.

Starfish cling to rocks with a sigh,
As the water laps gently around,
Each tidal whisper seems to imply,
That magic and wonder abound.

The flicker of fish darts and shimmers,
As if they know tales of the sea,
With every wave, the mystery glimmers,
Drawing our hearts to the deep blue lea.

So linger a while in this newfound realm,
Where mystery reigns and time stands still,
The shallow's allure, a magical helm,
Inviting us closer, with gentle thrill.

Breath of the Eldritch Waves

The ocean breathes in ancient ways,
Echoing far, where shadows merge,
With whispers of night that softly sways,
A mystical hymn, a serenade surge.

Its currents weave tales of forgotten lore,
Of creatures that glide in ghostly grace,
With each rise and fall, legends soar,
In the pulse of the deep, the hidden embrace.

Fathoms below, the lost sailors dream,
Cradled by waters, a tomb of rest,
Each ripple concealing secrets, it seems,
In darkness profound, their souls are blessed.

Yet among the foam, spells are cast,
As the moonlight weaves silvery strands,
A dance of horrors that shadows the past,
With each rolling wave, the mystery expands.

So heed the call of the eldritch sea,
Where time and reality intertwine,
For in its depths lies a curious key,
Unlocking realms where dreams align.

Chronicles of Blushing Sea Urchins

Among the rocks where the tides retreat,
Sea urchins blush in the warming sun,
Softly hiding their spiky feat,
As waves carry tales that they've spun.

Each little creature, a keeper of lore,
In the rhythm of sea, they sway and spin,
With colors bright, they softly implore,
The secrets they hold beneath their skin.

They sway like dancers, vibrant, bold,
Guardians of treasures unseen and rare,
In their prickly embrace, stories unfold,
Of tides and storms, of love and despair.

As the day dims, they gather in huddles,
Glistening shells catch the evening light,
Together they share in mischievous cuddles,
As shadows stretch, bidding farewell to night.

So take a moment by seaweed and rock,
To ponder their chronicles, wondrous and shy,
For within the tides, they defiantly flock,
With blushing hearts, the sea urchins lie.

9 781805 623878